YOU CHOOSE

AN INTERACTIVE ADVENTURE

CAN YOU BECOME A PRO GAMER?

BY ERIC BRAUN

CAPSTONE PRESS
a capstone imprint

Published by Capstone Press, an imprint of Capstone.
1710 Roe Crest Drive
North Mankato, Minnesota 56003
capstonepub.com

Library of Congress Cataloging-in-Publication Data
Names: Braun, Eric, 1971- author.
Title: Can you become a pro gamer? : an interactive adventure / by Eric Braun.
Description: North Mankato, Minnesota : Capstone Press, [2022] | Series: You choose: chasing fame and fortune | Includes bibliographical references. | Audience: Ages 8-12 | Audience: Grades 4-6 | Summary: "Can you hone your virtual gaming skills enough to make you a star in the world of pro gaming? First, find your game and pick your platform. Then, set out to see if you've got what it takes. Make real-life choices that can lead to disappointment, a future in the gaming industry, or realizing your dream of becoming king or queen of the console"—Provided by publisher.
Identifiers: LCCN 2021042199 (print) | LCCN 2021042200 (ebook) | ISBN 9781663958990 (hardcover) | ISBN 9781666323924 (paperback) | ISBN 9781666323931 (pdf)
Subjects: LCSH: Video gamers—Vocational guidance—Juvenile literature. | Video games industry—Juvenile literature.
Classification: LCC GV1469.3 .B73 2022 (print) | LCC GV1469.3 (ebook) | DDC 794.8092—dc23
LC record available at https://lccn.loc.gov/2021042199
LC ebook record available at https://lccn.loc.gov/2021042200

Editorial Credits
Editor: Mandy Robbins; Designer: Heidi Thompson; Media Researcher: Jo Miller; Production Specialist: Tori Abraham

Photo Credits
Getty Images: Cavan Images, 25, Complexio, 97, FOTOKITA, 83, gorodenkoff, 13, PhotoAttractive, 69, RyanKing999, 79, SeventyFour, 31, 63; Shutterstock: Dean Drobot, 73, Gorodenkoff, 20, 37, 64, Kichigin, 91, Parilov, 56, Pond Saksit, 42, Save nature and wildlife, Cover
Design Elements: Shutterstock: koltsovserezha, Nina_FOX, Southern Wind, Tetsuo Buseteru

TABLE OF CONTENTS

MAKING IT
BIG!

YOU have big dreams. You want to be the best gamer in the world! And you're willing to do whatever it takes to make your dream come true. But it's never a straight shot to the top, especially in the highly competitive gaming industry. Find out if you have what it takes to find fame and fortune as a pro gamer.

The first chapter sets the scene. Then you choose which path to read. Follow the directions at the bottom of each page. The choices you make will change your outcome. After you finish one path, go back and read the others for more adventures.

• Turn the page to begin your adventure.

YOU CHOOSE
THE PATH YOU TAKE TO
BECOME A
PRO GAMER.

DO YOU HAVE WHAT IT TAKES?

YOU are a video game star—at least in your own mind. You're good at action, role-playing, and strategy. You rock at sports games and puzzle games. You love to play solo, but you also love being part of a team.

• Turn the page.

Your best friend Bettina says you're the best gamer she knows—and she knows a lot of them. Bettina is a pretty great gamer herself. The two of you compete against each other and encourage each other. You make each other better, and you have fun doing it. You don't know what you'd do without her.

You tell Bettina that you're thinking of going pro, and she says you should go for it. "I'll help you," she says. "But it takes a ton of practice and hard work. Are you ready for that?"

"Oh, yeah," you tell her. "I am so ready."

The first thing you need to do is decide what game to specialize in. You could choose a well-known game that has been around a long time.

An established game like that will have lots of teams, lots of tournaments—and lots of prize money. The downside is that all that competition will make it hard to stand out in the crowd of players.

On the other hand, you could go with a newer game that's still gaining followers. There won't be as many competitions, and sponsors might not be ready to support players until the game is more popular. But you could quickly establish yourself as one of the top players. If the game does get big, you'll be ready to cash in.

"There's one other way you could go," Bettina says, smiling. "You could be a streamer." As a streamer, you wouldn't have to be the best. You'd just have to be entertaining.

• Turn the page.

You would have to be good enough that people would want to watch you play online. You'll have to work hard to earn subscribers and sponsors. It's a different way of going pro, but if you get enough fans, you can make a lot of money.

- To choose an established game, turn to page 15.
- To choose a new game, turn to page 45.
- To choose to be a streamer, turn to page 71.

INTO THE BLACK HOLE

Games don't get much more popular and well-established than *Black Hole Blitz*. It's also one of your favorite games. You've been playing it for years, and you've already got a pretty high ranking. With some dedicated practice, you are sure you can get good enough to go pro.

• Turn the page.

Black Hole Blitz is an action-adventure battle royale. The idea is that you and your team are on a spaceship that is damaged and gets sucked into a black hole. But instead of being crushed into oblivion, you find yourself transported to another universe—a universe at war.

The beings that live in this universe have destroyed their planets' environments through unlimited mining, building, and burning fuel. Resources like water, food, and fuel are scarce. You have to fight for them in order to survive.

Occasional gravity storms blow through, flattening the landscape and ripping apart shelters that are not built with Zorbitz. These tiny, highly magnetized marbles form an extremely powerful bond when combined. Naturally, the creatures of the black hole will kill each other for Zorbitz, just like they will for other resources.

Speaking of creatures, there are many alien beings here, including a few other humans who have fallen into the black hole. You have to watch out for giant worms, which burst out of the ground, fly through the air, and burrow back into the ground again. These creatures will eat any living thing they can catch, and that includes you. You also have to watch out for Limbagts—yellow ooze monsters that were brought to life from pollution in the oceans. Limbagts slither across the landscape in search of radioactive waste to feed on. Anything they touch will go up in flames.

You've played all the different roles in *Black Hole Blitz*, but you're best at being a warrior or a healer. If you want to go pro, you can't split your time practicing two different roles. You'll need to choose one to specialize in.

- To be a warrior, turn to page 18.
- To be a healer, turn to page 20.

Warriors are in the heart of the action, and that's what you like. Plus it's fun to blow stuff up.

You make a plan to practice eight hours a day, six days a week. It gets boring fast, but you stick with it. Bettina comes over some days and plays with you. She's good enough to challenge you and help you improve.

Before long, you're both rising in the league rankings. Bettina is lower than you, but she's still really good. She starts talking about going pro herself. She suggests that you, her, and a few of your other friends form your own team. She tells you this while the two of you are playing an online game against a couple of players who belong to a *Black Hole Blitz* team called the Fava Beans.

The game is close, but in the end, one of the Fava Beans blasts Bettina and takes her stash of Zorbitz. He quickly adds them to their shelter just before a devastating gravity storm comes through. Without those Zorbitz, you and Bettina are leveled in the storm. This swings the points advantage to the Fava Beans. When time runs out, they are the winners.

After the game, one of the Fava Beans messages you: "GG." You reply good game back to him. Then he says, "U shd try out for the FB."

He's inviting you to try out for the Fava Beans. This could be the opportunity you've been working for. Then you look over at Bettina.

- To try out for the Fava Beans, turn to page 23.
- To form a team with Bettina, turn to page 26.

Healers keep everyone on the team healthy. They also know how to turn Zorbitz into powerful shelters. They're the ones who can make important alliances. They make the big decisions for the team.

You begin practicing constantly. You watch streamers who play as healers to learn their tips and tricks. You also watch online tournaments to study your competition.

After a few months, your skills are razor sharp. You and Bettina join an online tournament with a big prize. To your surprise, you make it to the end! You're one of the last two teams. You recognize the tactic your opponent is using, and you know how to beat it. Calling out instructions to Bettina, you avoid a flying worm trap they'd set for you. Then you lure them into an open-air battle, where Bettina blows them away. You win!

Your phone blows up with messages. You and Bettina hug and soak in the glory. You'll be getting a pretty fat cash prize.

• Turn the page.

The next morning, you take a break from gaming to do some laundry and catch up on all those phone messages. Mixed in with all the congratulations, you have two messages from pro scouts. They're impressed by your team, but especially by you. Both invite you to join their teams. Bettina is understanding. After all, she was just playing to help you go pro. She's not sure she's ready yet.

The Space Frogs are a scrappy young team that's been getting a lot of buzz lately. You would get to represent them in tournaments right away. Cosmic Slop, on the other hand, is a larger, older team with more money and fancy gear. It might be nice to play for a rich team like that, but it could take a while to work your way up their system.

- To play for the Space Frogs, turn to page 28.
- To play for Cosmic Slop, turn to page 30.

You love Bettina and your other friends. It sounds really fun to form a team with them. But deep down, you don't think they can go all the way. If you want to succeed as a pro, you have to join a real team. You accept the invitation to try out for the Fava Beans.

The tryout is online. You stream with members of the Beans while you play. They put you through some drills and ask you lots of questions about your playing style and your strengths and weaknesses. After a couple hours, it's over. Later that night, you get a phone call.

"Hey, this is Barry from the Beans. We'd like to invite you to join the team."

You can hardly believe your ears. "Thanks," you manage to mutter.

• Turn the page.

That summer, you travel with the team to Las Vegas for a huge live tournament. As you're about to take your seats, Barry tells you that the Fava Beans have made a secret agreement with a top-ranked team, Cosmic Slop.

Your job is to leave some Zorbitz in a hiding spot in a busted-out old farm shed, where a Slop player will find them. Those Zorbitz will be the key to pushing Cosmic Slop to the highest point total in the tournament. Then the Slop will secretly help the Fava Beans so your team will at least come in the top five. Wherever you finish, Cosmic Slop has agreed to split the prize money with your team equally.

A win would boost their ranking and help with sponsorships. If the Beans come in the top five, it will be a big boost to your up-and-coming team too.

This type of deal is against the rules. If anyone finds out, your team loses eligibility for a year. So will every individual player who cheated. On the other hand, if you pull it off, you get money! Your team will skyrocket up the rankings, and your career will take off with it.

- To tell Barry you won't do it, turn to page 32.
- To go along with the plan, turn to page 34.

If you make it big, you want to make it with your friends by your side. You message back to the Fava Beans, "No thx." Then you put your controller down and tell Bettina you want to form a team with her.

Her smile tells you that you made the right choice. You and Bettina pull in five other friends and begin to work.

You practice together every day. Things are going great. You've known each other for a long time and get along well. You share old jokes and listen to music. Practices take on a party atmosphere. But people are spending more time goofing off than they are practicing. One of your teammates keeps asking about getting cool uniforms. You tell him your team has to earn some money before you can afford cool uniforms.

Then one of your friends drops out because he needs to work more. "I gotta pay rent," he says.

Your team isn't winning any tournaments or games, and you're definitely not getting any attention from sponsors. It takes a lot more discipline to make it as pro gamers than this team is willing to put in.

On the other hand, this is the most fun you've had in your life. You look at Bettina and a couple other friends laughing while they play. Bettina is laughing so hard she got the hiccups. You start to laugh too.

Okay, so maybe you won't make it big. As long as you can make enough to survive, you are okay with that.

--- THE END ---

To follow another path, turn to page 12.
To learn more about becoming a pro gamer, turn to page 103.

The Space Frogs take you in as one of their own. They demand even more practice time than you are used to. They teach you some skills drills that you never tried before. Your in-game action improves. Your ranking in league play climbs even higher than it was.

As time goes by, the team depends on you more and more. You've proven that you know where to be when someone needs healing. You always find more resources than anyone else. You consistently seem to know the other team's strategy.

You begin to lose touch with Bettina, but you grow closer with your teammates. You're starting to think of the Space Frogs as more of a family than a team. Then one day you get a text from a scout from another—better—team.

The Space Frogs are no longer climbing up. Prize money is not growing. So you decide to take the new team's offer. You say goodbye to the Space Frogs and start making friends on your new team. You're making more money now, but already you can tell that you'll rise to the top of this team too. Then what? You'll have to go to yet another team. Again, you'll make more money, but you'll leave more friends behind again.

The money is nice. So is the fame—gamers everywhere know your name. But you also feel lonely. You start to wonder: Is it worth it?

--- THE END ---

To follow another path, turn to page 12.
To learn more about becoming a pro gamer, turn to page 103.

Cosmic Slop's first assignment for you is to watch lots of competitor videos and livestreams and write up reports. You spend two weeks watching everything they ask you to, carefully taking notes. When it's time for the team to enter a tournament, they ask you to brief the team members who will be competing. Obviously, you will not be competing. After all, you've barely practiced over the past two weeks.

With your research to help them, the team does well. It comes in third in the tournament. "You did such a great job," the captain, Raz, tells you. He asks you to scout for the next tournament too, and the one after that.

As time goes by, you start to lose patience. You're spending so much time scouting, your skills are getting rusty. You text Raz about it. "When can I compete?"

"Don't worry," he texts back.

Sitting alone in your room with a list of tournament videos to watch, it dawns on you that you're miserable. But what choice do you have? You may never get another shot to join a team this good.

- To quit the team, turn to page 35.
- To stick it out, turn to page 36.

"Barry," you say. "I'm not sure about this."

"Don't worry," he assures you. "It's going to work out great."

Out in the arena, the music gets louder. Fans begin to cheer, as teams start taking their stations. Your stomach fills with a buzzing feeling. You think of Bettina, and how much she believes in you. How disappointed she would be if she knew you cheated.

"Sorry, Barry," you say. "I won't do it."

Barry gives you a stern look. "Okay," he says. For a second you think he means "okay" as in the plan is off. But then he says, "You're off the team." He calls a different team member over to take your place in the tournament.

You can't believe it. It happened so fast. Your dream seems to be dead just like that.

You go straight to Bettina's apartment. She lets you in and sees that you're upset.

"What happened?" she asks.

"I don't want to talk about it," you say. "Wanna' play something?"

"Sure," she says. "*Black Hole Blitz?*"

"No. Anything but that," you say.

It's good to know you'll always be welcome at Bettina's.

--- THE END ---

To follow another path, turn to page 12.
To learn more about becoming a pro gamer, turn to page 103.

You don't feel right about it, but you go along with the plan. It works! Cosmic Slop picks up the Zorbitz you hid for them, and it pushes them to victory.

The Fava Beans take third and make a big jump in worldwide standings. You get a new sponsor and more ads on your videos. That means more money. It also means tougher competition for your daily games. Your team continues to break the rules, making shady deals with other teams. You're starting to feel really guilty about it. This isn't the way you wanted to make it to the top. You can't go on like this. You feel awful.

The team is going to travel to another tournament out of state. It's an important one, with big cash prizes at stake. You're not sure you want to do it anymore.

- To stay home while the rest of the team travels, turn to page 37.
- To go to the tournament, turn to page 39.

You text back to Raz: "Sry, I'm out."

Back on your own again, you double down on practice time. You play up to 13 hours a day. You are determined to find another team—a team that wants you to play.

After a few weeks, you're playing the best you ever have, and another team notices. They invite you to join them, and you do. They ask if you want to play in an online tournament this coming weekend. Of course you do—this is what you've been working for. But you promised Bettina you'd play frisbee golf with her on Saturday. You don't want to let her down. But you're finally on a team that wants you to play! Bettina would understand . . . maybe.

- To play frisbee golf with Bettina, turn to page 41.
- To go to the tournament, turn to page 43.

It's hard to get on a pro team. It's extra hard to get on a top team like Cosmic Slop. You decide you better stick with them.

But Raz keeps making you scout. When you ask to play more, he tells you to be a team player. You try, but you're not having fun anymore. One day, you take a break from scouting opponents' livestreams and watch some other videos. You find a channel for a guitar player about your age. His songs are good, and he has lots of subscribers. He has ads on his videos, which means he's making some money. Most important, he looks happy.

You tell Raz you quit. You don't want to be a gamer anymore.

Raz just laughs. "What are you gonna do?" he asks.

"I don't know," you reply. "Maybe I'll be a musician."

--- THE END ---

To follow another path, turn to page 12.
To learn more about becoming a pro gamer, turn to page 103.

You decide to stay home and focus on your well-being. With all of your time focused on gaming, you haven't been eating properly or exercising for a while. You cook healthy meals instead of ordering takeout. You add a daily run to your routine. And you start getting more sleep.

• Turn the page.

You start thinking seriously about your future in gaming. You wonder if any of the teams actually play fairly. Does everyone cheat to get ahead? You also realize that only a lucky few gamers make enough money to live well on. And you're not sure you will ever get there.

After playing with the Fava Beans for more than a year, you decide to quit—not just the team, but pro gaming altogether. You get a job as a gaming coach at a camp for younger players. When you play on your own, it's just for fun. And that's the best part—gaming is fun again.

--- THE END ---

To follow another path, turn to page 12.
To learn more about becoming a pro gamer, turn to page 103.

You feel pressured by your team to go to the tournament. They need you to take part in another backhanded deal that's against the rules. Except this time you get caught!

The Fava Beans are disqualified, and you're kicked out of gaming for a year. On the drive home from the tournament Barry takes a call from your biggest sponsor. They are thinking about dropping their sponsorship. You listen to Barry tell the sponsor that you were the only player involved in the cheating scandal, and he can trust the rest of them.

You're beyond enraged! You knew it was wrong to cheat all along. You never would have done it if it wasn't for them! You should have followed your gut instincts. Your time as a professional gamer is over.

• Turn the page.

A month later, the Beans get caught in yet ANOTHER cheating scandal. The team is forced to disband altogether. You're not surprised, and you don't feel bad for them one bit.

--- THE END ---

To follow another path, turn to page 12.
To learn more about becoming a pro gamer, turn to page 103.

You go to the park with your friends. It's a beautiful day, and you have a great time. Afterward, you all get takeout and eat it at your place. Someone finds the tournament streaming online. Your new team is doing well.

"It looks like they might get into the top five," Bettina says. "Sorry you missed it."

"Don't be," you say. "I had a great day."

You stick with your new team for a few weeks after that, but more and more, you'd rather be hanging out with your friends. Eventually you decide that you don't have the dedication it takes to be a pro gamer. You didn't realize how much of your life you'd have to give up. You quit the team and take a job as a cook in the restaurant where Bettina works.

• Turn the page.

You may not have fulfilled your dream of being a pro gamer, but you're happier than you've been in months.

--- THE END ---

To follow another path, turn to page 12.
To learn more about becoming a pro gamer, turn to page 103.

Sure, you're burned out. Sure, you'd love to hang out with your friends. Sure, playing in the park sounds amazing. But you're a pro gamer. You're part of a team.

So you go to the tournament. You're focused and aggressive. You play better than you ever have. The team places fourth—their best finish ever. The difference was you. Soon, as the team keeps rising in the worldwide rankings, you become a team captain. You get sponsorships from major brands. You start winning tournaments. You are making good money.

And then, almost before you realize it, you are making really good money. You move out of your apartment into a house and buy a new car. You haven't seen Bettina in months, but you're playing a game you love and making a good living. Your persistence has paid off. You are a top-notch pro gamer.

--- THE END ---

To follow another path, turn to page 12.
To learn more about becoming a pro gamer, turn to page 103.

FIRED UP AND KICKIN' OFF

You've been getting really into this new game called *Jet Slinger*. It's like soccer in a stadium with a three-story ceiling and characters wearing jetpacks.

The game is played mostly above the ground. You can play as a human, which tends to be quicker and more agile. Or you can play as a Kruper. This big, hulking creature is slower than humans. But it kicks the ball with such powerful force that you can't block it with just one human. So far, *Jet Slinger* hasn't gotten very popular, but you think it will catch on.

• Turn the page.

You begin a strict daily practice routine. First thing in the morning, you spend two hours on mechanics—repetitive drills to improve your reactions and fine skills specific to the game.

Then you move on to two hours of shooting drills. You take shot after shot on goal against different bot goalies. After a short break to stretch your legs and eat, you devote four hours to scrimmaging online. This gives you a chance to improve your overall game play, as well as scout who else out there is getting good at *Jet Slinger*. Every night you watch other players' streams for at least two hours.

Everything is going great. You're getting better, and the game is starting to get more popular. There's one problem, though. As your skills improve, you outgrow your equipment.

Your PC isn't fast enough to keep up with your moves, and your internet sometimes lags. That can cost you a game when you're playing against tough competition.

The Shasta Tournament is in two weeks. If you keep practicing hard until then, you might be good enough to win it. The prize money would be enough to replace your PC. On the other hand, you could pick up some extra shifts at the café where you work. After a few weeks, you'd probably have enough money to upgrade your system.

- To focus on the Shasta Tournament, turn to page 48.
- To earn money for a new PC, turn to page 50.

Working extra shifts means less time for practicing *Jet Slinger*, and you don't want to slow down on your progress right now. You've been playing really well. You want to keep getting better. Besides, there's another online player named Pico who you really want to catch. You've played him a number of times, and he almost always beats you. Then he teases you about it in the chat. You'd really like to pass him in the rankings.

As the Shasta Tournament draws near, however, Pico keeps beating you. After one game, he messages you, "UR gonna bomb at Shasta!"

Anger blazes inside of you, but a small cloud of doubt is also creeping in. Pico might be right. You will have to place in the top 20 to win a cash prize.

Even the 20th-place prize would be enough
to upgrade your PC. But if you don't win a prize,
you will have lost your entry fee. Maybe you
should skip it.

- To enter the Shasta Tournament, turn to page 52.
- To wait for a later tournament, when you're better, turn to page 55.

You can't go pro with lousy equipment. You work all your regular shifts at the café, and you pick up other shifts every chance you get. Many days, you work from open to close. You keep practicing *Jet Slinger* when you can fit it in, to keep your skills sharp.

One day, you're carrying out a tray of food and bump into Bettina, who also works there. The food topples to the floor.

"Sorry," Bettina says. "Let me help you clean up."

"You're so clumsy!" you snap. "I can't stand it."

Bettina's face turns red as she walks back into the kitchen. Customers are looking at you. You are shocked. Where did that come from? Bettina is your best friend. You have never said a mean word to her in your life.

That's when you realize that you're exhausted. You have been working and gaming so much, you're barely sleeping at night. And you were a total jerk to Bettina. You feel terrible.

After work, you step outside into the cool night air. You're desperate to go home and get some sleep, but you also know you need to talk to Bettina. A text message is not going to do it. You need to apologize in person.

- To go to Bettina's place, turn to page 57.
- To go home now and see Bettina tomorrow when you're in a better state of mind to talk, turn to page 61.

You've been training for this tournament for a long time. You're not going to back out now.

In the week leading up to the big day, you practice even more than usual. You are feeling confident as you check into the tournament website on the big day. Your first game is against an unranked player. You beat him easily. Your next matchup is slightly tougher, but you win that one too. You win your third and fourth games.

Your fifth game is against Jetgirl. You've played her before. You're pretty evenly matched. The two of you play an intense game, but she wins it when her Kruper blasts a last-second goal from midfield. If you lose again, you'll be eliminated.

While you're waiting for your next game, you get up and stretch. Your computer chimes, alerting you that your next matchup is set.

The game will start in two minutes. You look at the scoreboard to see who your opponent is. Your heart starts thumping hard. It's Pico.

He's the one player who really gets under your skin. You can't let his trash talk bother you, or you will get flustered and make mistakes.

Like you, Pico has had one loss. The loser of this game will be eliminated, while the winner is one step closer to the prize money. Thirty seconds before the opening whistle, Pico pops a message up on screen: "Good luck."

What's that supposed to mean? Is he trolling you? The whistle sounds, and you have the kickoff. You move a human character downfield and pass to a Kruper. The Kruper kicks it off the ceiling so it bounces right back to your human.

• Turn the page.

You aim it at the goal and score! You start to relax a little.

Unfortunately, that's the only goal you get the whole game. Pico scores one to tie it. Then late in the fourth quarter the worst possible thing happens—your PC lags. Pico's player gets past your defender and scores the winning goal.

--- THE END ---

To follow another path, turn to page 12.
To learn more about becoming a pro gamer, turn to page 103.

There will be more tournaments. Why pay to play in one now when you aren't sure you can do well? It makes more sense to keep practicing.

The night of the tournament, you and Bettina go to a movie. It feels nice to think about something besides *Jet Slinger*. You go home and get a good night's sleep.

When you wake up the next morning, you have a text message from Pico: "Y did you skip Shasta? U could have done well."

You are surprised. Maybe all that teasing was just in fun. Maybe he really thinks you're good at *Jet Slinger*. You text back to ask how he did. He tells you that he finished in the top 20—good enough to take home some prize money. Then he says, "I got a sponsor and am forming a *Jet Slinger* team. Wanna join?"

• Turn the page.

Being on a sponsored team would be great. It would be a big step toward making it as a pro gamer. But you can't help wondering if he's serious. Is this another joke at your expense?

- To join Pico's team, turn to page 62.
- To decline Pico's offer, turn to page 64.

Bettina's friendship is more important than any amount of sleep. You ride your bike to her apartment and knock on the door. She answers in her pajamas. The TV is on in the background.

"What do you want?" she says, rubbing her eye sleepily.

"I want to apologize," you say. "I acted like a jerk."

"Yeah," she says. "You did."

"I didn't mean it," you say. "You're not clumsy. The accident was my fault. I'm working too much, and I'm not sleeping. I'm tired and cranky all the time, and I took it out on you. I'm really sorry."

She stands there a moment. You can't tell if she's going to accept your apology or not.

• Turn the page.

Finally, she steps aside. "You want to come in?"

"I would love to," you say. You sit on the couch with her and watch a movie. You fall asleep before it ends. You wake up in the morning on her couch with a blanket over you.

Bettina makes scrambled eggs for breakfast. As you're eating, she says, "You know, I have a lot of money saved up. I could lend you what you need for a new PC. You can pay me back later. Then you don't have to work so much."

You accept Bettina's loan and buy a new computer and a faster monitor. Right away, you start winning more games. Just having reactions that are a fraction of a second faster makes a huge difference. Soon, you are one of the top 100 players in the world.

A candy brand offers to sponsor you, and you accept. The sponsorship money is not enough to live on, but it does let you work fewer hours at the café and spend more time gaming. Soon, you get the attention of another sponsor that makes gaming chairs, and they sign on with you.

You become friends with two other players online. The three of you form a team called the Exploding Dragon Babies—EDB for short. Together, you enter a three-on-three tournament. Many of the best players in the world are in. EDB makes an impressive third-place finish.

Third place comes with a cash prize, so you repay Bettina the money she lent you plus a little extra. But all is not well. You've been so busy with EDB that you totally forgot to go to work twice last week. Your boss calls you up to fire you.

• Turn the page.

You have a decision to make. Your sponsorships are nice, but they're still not enough to live on. You need a part-time job to pay your expenses. Either that, or you can throw yourself into *Jet Slinger* full time and see if you can land more sponsors.

- To look for another job, turn to page 66.
- To play *Jet Slinger* full time, turn to page 68.

You really need some rest. Then you'll talk to Bettina. So you go home and sleep for 12 hours. When you wake up, you turn on your computer to play a little *Jet Slinger* before heading over to Bettina's place. You're on a good run, beating some tough players online, so you keep playing.

But then your computer glitches at a bad moment, and you give up a goal. You're so mad that you throw your controller—and it hits your monitor. The monitor glass is spiderwebbed, making it useless.

That's when you realize you've been playing *Jet Slinger* for five hours, and you still haven't apologized to Bettina. Gaming is getting in the way of what is really important—the people you care about. You turn off your computer and head over to her apartment. You hope she accepts your apology.

--- THE END ---

To follow another path, turn to page 12.
To learn more about becoming a pro gamer, turn to page 103.

Why not give it a shot? You text back that you're interested.

Over the next few weeks, you and Pico video chat several times. He's actually a really nice guy. He apologizes for all the mean comments. "Sometimes I try to be funny, but it comes across as mean."

You practice together and play as partners against other teams. Your sponsor, a PC company, replaces your old equipment with the fastest gear available. It makes a big difference. As *Jet Slinger* becomes more popular, you and Pico are among the best players there are. Soon, the tournaments start to have bigger prizes. *Jet Slinger* becomes one of the most popular games in the world, and you and Pico are taking home huge prizes. With the help of someone you had thought was your enemy, you've made your dream of becoming a pro gamer come true!

--- THE END ---

To follow another path, turn to page 12.
To learn more about becoming a pro gamer, turn to page 103.

You don't trust Pico—he has trash talked you for too long. Besides, even if this is not a joke, do you really want to be on a team with such a jerk?

You tell him thanks, but no thanks, and keep playing on your own. You hope that a real team will notice your talent and invite you to join them.

Unfortunately, it doesn't happen. You don't get a sniff of attention from any teams. Meanwhile, Pico recruits a few other players for his team, LazerBrain. They're good. You can only watch as they win games and tournaments and slowly rise to the top of the *Jet Slinger* world.

--- THE END ---

To follow another path, turn to page 12.
To learn more about becoming a pro gamer, turn to page 103.

You find a job loading boxes at a fulfillment center for an online retailer. You spend your shifts in a huge warehouse. You drive a forklift and take products down from tall shelves and then pack them into boxes. It is boring, but you can make your own schedule. You work just enough to get by and spend the rest of your time gaming.

Your team gets better, and you even place high enough in a couple of tournaments to take home some prize money. But after a year and a half, nothing has really changed. You still have to work in the warehouse to make ends meet. You still win very little money in tournaments, and sometimes you don't place at all. You can't seem to break through to the next level where you're actually winning and making good money. It feels like you're spinning your wheels.

At the same time, you have made some good friends at the fulfillment center where you work. Your boss has offered you a raise and a promotion to manager, but you'd have to work full time. You realize that something has changed for you. Surprisingly, you like your job and the friends you've made there more than you like gaming. You tell your teammates that you're dropping out of pro gaming. You take the promotion.

--- THE END ---

To follow another path, turn to page 12.
To learn more about becoming a pro gamer, turn to page 103.

Now is the time to go for it. If you're going to be a successful pro gamer, you have to give it your best shot.

You and your teammates meet online to practice every day. You also practice on your own. You study other players, watch tournaments, and work on new plays to use with your teammates. It all comes together pretty well. Soon, between sponsorships and tournament winnings, you are making enough money that you don't need a "real" job. You're not going to get rich—it doesn't seem like you team has enough talent to reach the highest levels—but you enjoy the lifestyle. You play games for a living. You meet interesting people from all over the world. You occasionally travel for live tournaments, spending time in new cities. You're not a star, but you're happy.

--- THE END ---

To follow another path, turn to page 12.
To learn more about becoming a pro gamer, turn to page 103.

LOOK AT ME!

You already have a few hundred followers on your video channel, where people can watch you play video games. If those people wanted to learn tips and tricks to get better at gaming, there are better players they could watch. The reason they click on your videos is because they think you're entertaining. You're funny. You also tie in smart observations about current events and news.

• Turn the page.

So what's the difference between the videos you're doing now and going pro as a livestreamer? Mostly, it's quantity. Right now, you post maybe two or three times a month, and it's not all gaming videos. You might have an idea for a prank, or you might want to shoot a bike jump or part of your camping trip. But to build a fan base as a gaming streamer, you'll have to do videos and livestreams, and you'll have to do them every day. You'll need to create a lot of content so that people will keep coming back to your channel.

You can do this!

You can make money from people tipping you, or giving donations. You can charge a small fee for subscribers. There are also advertisements and affiliate links who might pay you. Affiliate links take viewers to their products. If your viewers buy their products, you get some of the money.

To start off, you buy a nice headset with a high-quality microphone. You get rid of the clothing hooks hanging behind your seat and paint the wall black. Now the background behind you will be plain and not distracting. You decide the built-in camera in your computer is good enough—no need to upgrade that.

• Turn the page.

Now you need to decide on a persona, or personal style. That way, people will know what to expect, and they will know they can rely on you. If you usually do funny posts but then one day start posting angry videos about politics, you'll lose subscribers. Consistency is key.

You talk about it with Bettina, and the two of you come up with two ideas. One is to use your sense of humor to be a joking, trash-talking goofball. "Or you could be more of a social commentator," Bettina says. "You care about a lot of social issues, and you have good ideas. People might like the more sincere side of you."

- To take the goofball route, turn to page 75.
- To be a sincere social commentator, turn to page 78.

Bettina helps you write some material. You have topics and a basic outline to discuss for each of the first 14 days. You don't write out a script because you can't read while you're playing video games. But you map out what you want to say, and you memorize a few funny phrases and jokes.

For the first three days, you talk almost exclusively about eating in public. Some people are really insecure and barely eat in public. But other people are disgusting. You spend almost an hour telling a story about a man you saw at a restaurant who picked his nose at the table. You stretch out the story, adding lots of disgusting details. You describe the man's wife who was at the table and how he was hiding his nose-picking from her.

• Turn the page.

All the while, you are playing your favorite action battle game, *Flaming Fists of Fury (FFF)*. Sometimes you take a break from your stories to comment on what's happening in the game. "I've been trying to beat this guy all week, and he's driving me crazy. See, watch this. I'll come in with a Roasting Roundhouse and he . . . ugh, see? He got me again. Anyway, so this guy is now literally wiping cheese out of the middle of his grilled cheese sandwich with the same finger he was digging for gold with just a second ago . . ."

You meet with Bettina regularly, and she tells you the booger-picker story was great. As word gets out about your videos, you start to gain followers. You're getting some encouraging feedback in the comments section. But after the two weeks of planned material ends, you find it harder to come up with stuff to say.

Instead of posting every day, you start skipping days. This is not a good idea if you are trying to grow your follower count. You're going to need more ideas for content.

"You know," you say to Bettina, "some streamers get really popular by feuding with other streamers. I could start a feud—that would be fun."

Bettina makes a face like she's not so sure she likes that idea. But you've seen it work before.

- To start a feud with another streamer, turn to page 81.
- To brainstorm other ideas with Bettina, turn to page 84.

You love to joke around, but you have a serious side too. You care about politics, and you want to make the world a better place. If you can make a living as a livestreaming pro gamer while doing it, that sounds good to you.

A politician you admire is caught cheating on his taxes, and you discuss this during one of your livestreams. You feel let down by this man. He says he didn't cheat—he just made a mistake. But you think he's smarter than that. It wasn't a mistake.

Talking about why you used to support him, and what it means that he doesn't pay his taxes leads you to discuss other topics. You go on to talk about the importance of taxes in supporting a fair and healthy community.

Later that week, you tell a story about an ice cream truck vendor who lost her license after someone got sick from one of her treats. The week after that, things get a bit more serious. You start talking about an upcoming election and what you think of the candidates. This discussion earns you lots of new followers—and also lots of hate mail.

• Turn the page.

People who disagree with you start leaving nasty comments on your channel and sending you vicious emails. They find you on social media too. You even get some threats. You defend yourself on social media, and this spikes your follower count even more. But the angry comments are starting to get to you.

- To be less controversial in your videos in hopes that people will leave you alone, turn to page 86.
- To keep doing what you're doing, turn to page 88.

There's a very popular streamer who also plays *FFF*. Her name is Hazel, and she often spends time in her livestreams making fun of other streamers. She's famous for her hilarious and creative takedowns of other gamers. Tangling with her could be risky if she makes you look ridiculous. But getting her to talk about you on her gamecast would be amazing publicity.

So you watch a couple of her livestreams and notice that she's getting downright mean. You decide to call her out on it. On your next stream, you call her a bully. You throw up some screen caps from her video and point out that she's actually not very good at *FFF*. You could beat her. Even a little kid could beat her. "So why is she so popular?" you ask your viewers. "She isn't any good at the game, and she's mean."

• Turn the page.

Your plan works—at first. Some of your viewers start tweeting about your video. Your subscriber count climbs. You get Hazel's attention too. She decides to make you the topic of her next livestream. She's probably grateful, you think. She probably has trouble coming up with content every day too. Now you'll both have something to talk about for a while as you stream your games.

Unfortunately for you, Hazel takes you down in a big way. She watches a couple of your videos and starts making fun of everything, from your voice to your haircut to the dumb (in her opinion) hot takes. Your comments section starts to get filled up with pro-Hazel comments. Your followers and subscribers start to abandon you. One former subscriber says, "Picking fights to be funny is not a good look." Hundreds of people give the comment a thumbs-up.

You never wanted to be a bully. You just wanted to have fun. You wanted to make a living playing a game you love. But it changed who you are. You became nasty and cruel—an online troll. You decide to give up being a streamer.

--- THE END ---

To follow another path, turn to page 12.
To learn more about becoming a pro gamer, turn to page 103.

"Would you help me?" you ask Bettina.

"Sure," she says. "I have some ideas."

The two of you spend the next few days brainstorming. Soon you have a list of topics and talking points to get you through the next month. While playing *FFF*, you joke about people who love cats. You explain your desire to carry grilled cheese sandwiches with you everywhere you go. You rant about dog owners who don't pick up their dog's poop. You're also getting really good at *FFF*. People are subscribing to your video channel for your gaming tips as well as your funny takes.

You decide to invite Bettina to be a guest on one of your livestreams. She is really funny, and the two of you have great compatibility. You get more tips, or donations, than ever before, so you invite her to guest again.

Once again, the two of you have a great time. Your number of subscribers goes up by 20 percent in one week, and the tips keep rolling in.

- To invite Bettina to be a permanent part of the team, turn to page 90.
- To keep going it alone, turn to page 92.

It is exhausting and painful being trolled all the time. So you decide to tone down your content a little bit. Maybe if you are less controversial, the trolling will stop.

For the next couple weeks, you focus on less fiery topics. For two days, you talk about how terrible it is that plastic pollution is filling the oceans. Ocean creatures are seeing their habitat destroyed. How can anyone argue with that?

Your plan works. The controversy dies down, and the trolling mostly ends. Unfortunately, you lose both haters and followers. Your subscriber count goes down. You try to drum up support on social media, but you seem to be stuck.

Avoiding the hate mail and threats is worth it to you, so you keep doing it this way. Unfortunately, you can't make a living with this level of support from fans. But you have a decent number of subscribers who are loyal to you. Those subscriber fees are a nice addition to your part-time job at the café. You'll never be able to support yourself completely by streaming, but you're okay with that.

--- THE END ---

To follow another path, turn to page 12.
To learn more about becoming a pro gamer, turn to page 103.

It's no fun being threatened, that's for sure. But you are starting to make really good money, so you decide to keep talking about politics.

You spend several days playing *FFF* while talking about a particular politician you dislike. You roast him for his policies. You even go so far as to compare his face to a deflated chef's hat.

Your fans love it. The attacks and threats keep coming as well. You get more advertisers. So you keep it up.

Your gaming skills are also getting really good. You are attracting viewers who agree with your take on politics and love the game you play. These loyal fans are learning a lot about both from you.

Then one day you criticize a particular senator, in great detail. That night you get a message from one of your sponsors. They donate to the senator and are big supporters of hers. They say you need to tell your viewers you were wrong. You need to apologize to her in your video. If you don't, they will drop you.

This company brings in lots of money for you. It would hurt to lose them. But what would people think if you came out and apologized to this politician you obviously are against?

- If you decide to apologize, turn to page 94.
- If you refuse to apologize, turn to page 96.

You invite Bettina to join you as a partner. "We make a great team," you say. "We will be awesome together."

"I'm sorry," she says. "It's really fun for me to help you out sometimes, and I enjoy being a guest. But I don't want to do this as my job. I already have a job I really like."

You're disappointed, but you keep on working at being a pro streamer. You have some great days, where your videos are funny and insightful and get shared on social media a lot. You also have some duds, which is okay. You can't be perfect all the time. After a while, though, the duds start to outnumber the great days. Without Bettina, you're not as good. And it's not as fun. It's not worth all the work you're putting into it.

Your favorite part of being a streamer was working as a team with Bettina. You decide to look into other careers that involve teamwork. In the meantime, you apply for a job at the café with Bettina.

--- THE END ---

To follow another path, turn to page 12.
To learn more about becoming a pro gamer, turn to page 103.

It's your dream to be a pro gamer, and you want to do it on your own. So you keep streaming every day. You're getting really good at it. You're finding it easier to create content, and you're having a good time.

As you gain more subscribers, a big video game maker called BloxConstrux starts advertising on your videos. You make a deal with them to try a new game they've created, and you include an affiliate link. Things seem to be on the upswing, but at a certain point your subscriber count stops growing. You need to find a way to spark new interest.

Lots of streamers host contests to gain followers. You could get some free games from your advertiser and offer them as prizes.

Another option would be to ask a popular streamer to guest star on each other's channels for a few days. This can be an easy way to gain exposure to new fans.

- To host a contest, turn to page 98.
- To ask another streamer to guest, turn to page 100.

You can't afford to lose your biggest advertiser. At the start of your next video you say, "Yesterday I said some stuff that was a little out of line." You talk about some of the senator's positions on important issues and how they're not that bad. Then you say, "I'm going to give her another chance, and I want to apologize to her."

You give a big smile to the camera, and then you go on with playing the game. You don't talk about her the rest of the video.

The reaction is immediate. Many of your fans are furious with you. They see it as selling out. They leave harsh comments, like, "I guess the money got to you, you fake!"

Angry fans drop their subscriptions. As you lose subscribers, you are less attractive to advertisers.

You keep the big advertiser, but with fewer subscribers, they pay you less money. You should have stuck to your guns. You might have lost one advertiser, but at least you'd have your self-respect and a lot more followers.

--- THE END ---

To follow another path, turn to page 12.
To learn more about becoming a pro gamer, turn to page 103.

Your viewers would know something is fishy if you suddenly changed your position about the senator. They would see through your lies, and you'd lose them as fans. You can't risk it.

Instead, you double down on the criticism. In your next three videos, you tear the senator's positions apart. Your biggest sponsor drops you, but you get more subscribers, and soon enough you get two new advertisers. The money is better than before.

One day, you are livestreaming a game of *FFF*, and your opponent starts leaving threatening comments in the chat. Without stopping your livestream, you call the police and report him. The cops end up arresting the person, who has threatened many others online. Your fans love it. Your popularity spikes.

You become rich and famous, playing video games on livestreams and talking about issues that are important to you. You're proud that your dreams have come true without you having to lose your integrity.

--- THE END ---

To follow another path, turn to page 12.
To learn more about becoming a pro gamer, turn to page 103.

You talk to BloxConstrux about hosting a contest. They agree to donate several copies of their new game, *Octopus Cops*. They also produce fancy gaming chairs. You convince them to donate one of those too.

You announce the contest on your livestream. To enter, people have to mention the contest and your streaming channel on social media and tag you. The interest builds slowly—not many people know about *Octopus Cops*. But over two weeks, a wave of entries builds. Hundreds of people are posting about your contest and your channel. It's incredible publicity. You keep streaming every day, talking about the contest, and continuing your witty banter. When the contest ends you give away the prizes.

Your follower count went up 20 percent during the contest, and you're making good money. Soon, though, people start posting reviews of *Octopus Cops*. Nobody likes it. It looks amazing—the visuals are gorgeous—but the game itself is boring. Many viewers begin to associate you with the boring game, and you get a reputation for being boring. You start losing subscriptions.

Once again, you'll have to come up with a new idea to attract new subs, and keep the ones you have. The best game streamers make it look so easy, but it's a ton of work. You believe in yourself, though. You'll keep adjusting. You won't give up.

--- THE END ---

To follow another path, turn to page 12.
To learn more about becoming a pro gamer, turn to page 103.

There's a streamer you like who plays *Black Hole Blitz*. You love that game, but you haven't played it since you started streaming. The streamer calls himself Starblazer. You decide to ask him to come on your channel to play *FFF* with you. Then you'll go on his channel to play *Black Hole Blitz*. It would be fun to watch two great gamers jump into different games and see what happens.

Starblazer likes the idea. You let your viewers know he'll be coming on. When he does, you have more viewers than ever before. He plays *FFF* with you, and the two of you have great banter. When you go on his channel to play *Black Hole Blitz*, it's similarly successful. You both get crossover subscribers to join your channels.

It is hard work coming up with content for your streams, but you seem to have a talent for it. People are interested in what you have to say. When you're streaming and talking to your fans, you feel like you're in the zone. Your ideas just flow. You keep getting bigger and bigger. The sky is the limit to how successful you'll become.

--- THE END ---

To follow another path, turn to page 12.
To learn more about becoming a pro gamer, turn to page 103.

LIFE IN THE GAME

Who wouldn't love to be paid to play their favorite game? But it's not as simple as just sitting around in your pajamas playing games. Becoming a pro gamer takes hard work and discipline. The good news is, it can be done. The idea of professional gaming used to seem odd, but over the last 10 years or so, it has become a real career.

The first step is choosing a game you're really good at. Then plan on practicing at least eight hours a day. That means doing drills, competing against other players online, and scouting other players. Many gamers hire a coach to help them get better quickly.

You will need high-quality equipment, including a powerful PC and a lightning quick monitor. If you want to compete at the highest level, this is really important. Next, get involved in the online community for your game. Make friends on social media, participate in chats, and develop a positive reputation. Just remember, people you meet online may not be who they say they are. As a rule, don't make plans to meet up with people you meet online. If someone makes you uncomfortable, block them. If someone makes you feel threatened, report them.

The next step is to find a team. If you're good enough, teams may let you try out. If you're really good, they may recruit you. Another option is to start your own team.

You can compete in leagues, which are a lot like other sports leagues. You play lots of games over the course of a season. You can also enter tournaments. These often come with big prize money.

Being a pro gamer means giving up the steady paycheck of a regular job. Instead, you are trying to win prize money. One way to balance out the dry spells between prizes is to get a sponsorship. If you are good enough, and you have a good reputation and lots of followers, a company may pay to advertise on your videos and streams. They may even pay you to use their gear when you're competing.

FAME OR FORTUNE
REALITY CHECK

GAMERS WITH THE MOST CAREER WINNINGS AS OF EARLY 2021:

Player name	Player ID	Career winnings
Johan Sundstein	NOtail	About $7 million
Jesse Vainikka	JerAx	About $6.5 million
Anathan Pham	ana	About $6 million

These include tournament winnings only. Many gamers add to their prize winnings by focusing on streaming. Streaming can earn gamers money through subscriptions, tips, affiliate links, and advertisements.

The tournament with the biggest prize pool is the International, a tournament that features the game DOTA 2. In 2021, the International had a total of $40.01 million in prizes up for grabs.

Twitch is a video-streaming platform popular with gamers. As of April 2021, the most popular content on Twitch was for the game *Grand Theft Auto V*. The next most popular game was *League of Legends*, followed by *Call of Duty: Modern Warfare*, *VALORANT*, and *Minecraft*.

To succeed as a pro gamer, it pays have to have very strong basic gaming skills. But every game has its own unique mechanics. Once you choose a game to specialize in, practice the specific mechanics for that game over and over.

OTHER PATHS TO EXPLORE

Gaming wouldn't be possible without game developers. What would you rather do—be a gamer or create the games? Why?

What are some ways that being a pro gamer is different from other kinds of jobs? Do those differences sound appealing to you? Why or why not?

It can be hard to balance a demanding job with a social life, and sometimes close friends drift apart. Do you think it's worth it to make this sacrifice? Why or why not?

GLOSSARY

affiliate link (uh-FIL-ee-et LINK)—a link on someone's site to an advertiser's website; if a viewer clicks the link, the advertiser knows that the person came to their website from the affiliate's website, and if a sale is made, the affiliate gets part of the sale

battle royale (BAT-uhl roy-AL)—an online, multiplayer game that involves both fighting and survival game types, where the "last man standing" wins

livestream (LIVE-streem)—to broadcast an event live over the internet

mechanics (muh-CAN-iks)—the specific actions gamers use to achieve results in a game

streamer (STREEM-ur)—a person who posts videos and livestreams of content they create for others to view

SELECTED BIBLIOGRAPHY

Intel: How to Become a Pro Gamer in 10 Steps
intel.com/content/www/us/en/gaming/resources/want-pro-gamer.
html

Steel Series: How to Become a Professional Gamer
steelseries.com/blog/how-to-become-a-professional-gamer-93

Techni Sport: How to Become a Pro Gamer in 2021
technisportusa.com/blogs/news/how-to-become-a-pro-gamer

READ MORE

Braun, Eric. *Can You Become a Social Media Influencer?* North Mankato, MN: Capstone, 2022.

Mauleón, Daniel. *Esports Revolution.* North Mankato, MN: Capstone, 2020.

Steele, Craig. *Ultimate Gamer: Career Mode: The Complete Guide to Starting a Career in Gaming.* New York: Kingfisher, 2021.

INTERNET SITES

BluHazy
twitch.tv/bluhazy

eSports Lane
esportslane.com

GamerGirl
youtube.com/channel/UCije75lmV_7fVP7m4dJ7ZoQ

ABOUT THE AUTHOR

Eric Braun is a children's author and editor.
He has written dozens of books on many topics,
and one of his books was read by an astronaut on
the International Space Station for kids on Earth to
watch. Eric lives in Minneapolis with his wife, two
kids, and a dog who is afraid of cardboard.